A DK PUBLISHING BOOK
www.dk.com

Editor Lara Tankel Holtz
Art Editor Diane Thistlethwaite
Additional Design Assistance
Helen Melville and Jacqueline Gooden
Deputy Managing Editor Dawn Sirett
Deputy Managing Art Editor Jane Horne
Picture Research Monica Allende
Production Ruth Cobb

Consultant Jane Bunting
Photography Norman Hollands

Additional photography Paul Bricknell, Jane Burton,
Gordon Clayton, Mike Dunning, Steve Gorton,
Colin Keates, Dave King, Cyril Laubscher,
Richard Leeney, Mike Linley, Stephen Oliver,
Steve Shott, and Jerry Young.

First American Edition, 1998
4 6 8 10 9 7 5 3

Published in the United States by DK Publishing, Inc.,
95 Madison Avenue, New York, New York 10016

Photographs: gecko page 14 copyright © 1991 Jerry Young;
butterfly page 10, moth page 13, and rhinoceros page 18
copyright © 1992 Jerry Young

The publisher would like to thank the following for
their kind permission to reproduce their photographs:
(c=center, BC=back cover)

Britstock-IFA: 15c West Stock Everton grass; **Robert Harding:**
18c elephants, 19c ballet dancers; **Images:** 10c sailing boat,
17c lavender; **Telegraph:** 11c children with kite, 14c D.Norton field,
16c F.P.G.D. & J. Gleiter sunset, 12c Subella trees, 20c Planet Earth
sky at night, 9c John Lythqoe sunflowers, 7c, BC Jan Tove Johansson
strawberries; **Tony Stone:** 21c Bob Torrez snow scene,
8c Shaun Egan bananas, 13c Art Wolfe bear.

Colors. -- 1st American ed.
          p. cm. -- (Play and learn concepts)
     Summary: Three fuzzy ducks introduce the concept of color.
     ISBN 0-7894-2912-8
     1. Colors--Juvenile literature. [1.Color.]   I. DK Publishing, Inc.
II. Series.
QC495.5.C642   1998
535.6--dc21
                                        97-38164
                                          CIP
                                          AC

Color reproduction by Colourscan, Singapore
Printed and bound in Italy by L.E.G.O.

Note to parents

In this book Dib, Dab, and Dob, the
playful ducks, help young children
to recognize a range of colors. There
are questions to ask on every page
that encourage children to talk
about colors and learn their names.
The pictures have been specially
chosen to appeal to young children.
Use them as a starting point and go
on to talk about the colors you see
in the world around you.

PLAY AND LEARN
COLORS

With Dib, Dab, and Dob

DK PUBLISHING, INC.

cherries

watermelon

Red

cap

roses

chilies

LADDER · NEW ROCHELLE

Dab wants to ride in a fire engine. Can you find two more red vehicles?

tomatoes

sports car

red
pepper

scissors

ribbon

candle

What's your
favorite
red fruit?

tractor

comb

Yellow

grapefruit

watering
can

daffodil

What yellow
fruit has Dab
slipped on?

canary

truck

cheese

cup

raincoat

sweet corn

lemon

Dob likes sunflowers. Can you name another yellow flower?

butterfly

toothbrush

Blue

waterproof boots

egg

spade

What blue things can Dab play with at the ocean?

bucket

paint

van

rope

bottle

sailboat

Dib flies her kite high in the sky. Is the sky always blue?

pencils

Brown

onions

teddy bear

nuts

What time of year do leaves turn brown?

hen

bread

Dib can see a big brown bear. Can you find another bear?

pinecone

feathers

moth

mushrooms

twig

pony

peas

Green

leaf

parrot

apple

broccoli

Are the leaves on trees always green?

gecko

caterpillar

frog

crayon

limes

kiwifruit

tree

What green plants can you see?

carrots

Orange

peaches

goldfish

crab

pumpkin

oranges

Dab is watching
the orange sunset.
When do you see
the sun set?

buttons

Purple

grapes

eggplant

flowers

glove

wool

Dib likes purple flowers. Where are the other flowers on this page?

pebbles

Gray

dolphin

clock

rabbit

rhinoceros

Can you find two
gray sea animals?

shark

pig

crayon

Pink

shell

hangers

hat

ice cream

Dib's favorite outfit
is her pink tutu.
What is yours?

ballet shoes

beetle

kitten

Black

plug

blackbird

olives

What can you
see in the black
sky at night?

shoe

chalk

golf
ball

White

polar bear

lamb

dove

cauliflower

toothpaste

Can you see a white
animal that likes the snow?

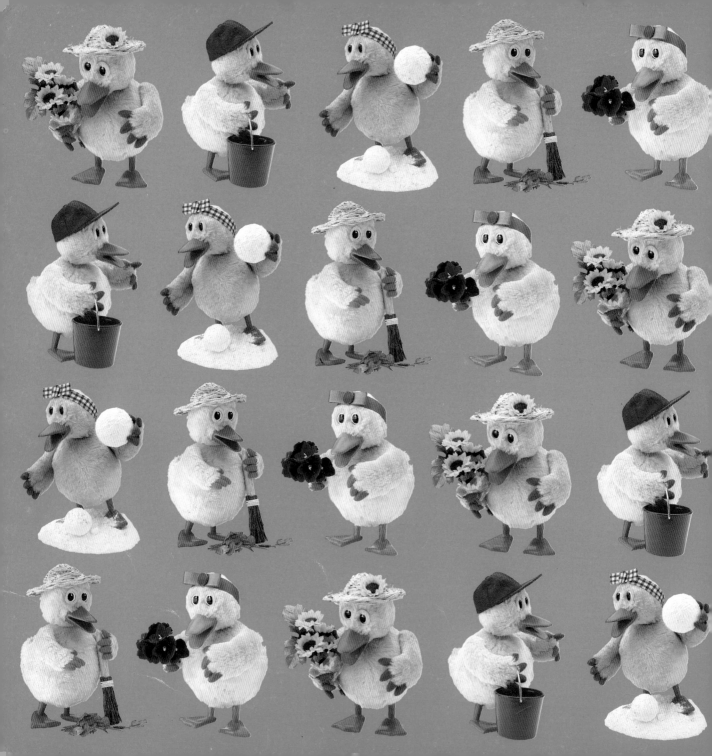